She Plays Softball

By Trudy Becker

level
2

little blue
readers

www.littlebluehousebooks.com

Copyright © 2023 by Little Blue House, Mendota Heights, MN 55120. All rights reserved. No part of this book may be reproduced or utilized in any form or by any means without written permission from the publisher.

Little Blue House is distributed by North Star Editions:
sales@northstareditions.com | 888-417-0195

Produced for Little Blue House by Red Line Editorial.

Photographs ©: Shutterstock Images, cover, 9 (top) , 9 (bottom), 10–11, 19 (top), 23 (top), 24 (top right), 24 (bottom left); iStockphoto, 4, 7, 12, 15, 19 (bottom), 21, 23 (bottom), 24 (top left); Pexels, 16, 24 (bottom right)

Library of Congress Control Number: 2022910480

ISBN
978-1-64619-711-8 (hardcover)
978-1-64619-743-9 (paperback)
978-1-64619-803-0 (ebook pdf)
978-1-64619-775-0 (hosted ebook)

Printed in the United States of America
Mankato, MN
012023

About the Author

Trudy Becker lives in Minneapolis, Minnesota. She likes exploring new places and loves anything involving books.

Table of Contents

Getting Ready

I play softball.

I love game days.

I get ready to play.

I find my uniform.

I wear pants and

long socks.

I wear a jersey too.

I put on my cap.

I put on my cleats too.

They help me run on

the dirt.

I need my softball bat to hit the ball.

I also grab my glove.

softball bat

glove

On the Field

Games happen at the softball field.

There are bases in the dirt.

In the middle is the pitching circle.

There is a green outfield too.

Before each game starts,

I find my position.

Sometimes I play in

the outfield.

I punch my glove to

get ready.

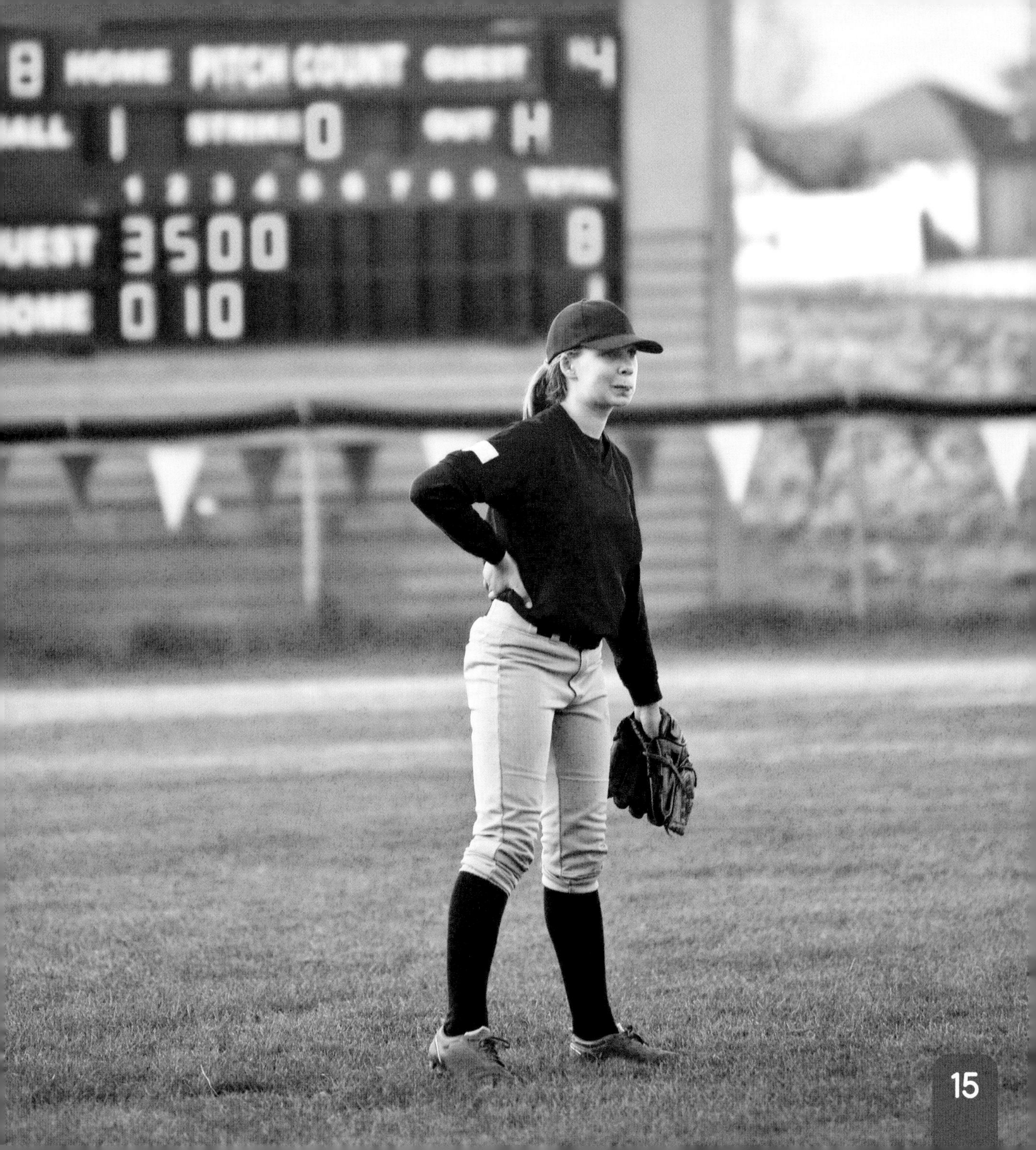
HOME
PITCH COUNT
GUEST

In the Game

I focus when the game starts.

Sometimes I am the pitcher.

I throw the ball hard over
the plate.

When a batter hits
the ball my way, I run
toward it.
I catch the ball in
my glove.
The batter is out!

Sometimes it is my turn to bat.

I swing at the pitch.

I drop the bat and run toward first base.

The ball flies over
the fence.
I hit a home run!
The crowd cheers, and I
run around the bases.
I love softball.

Glossary

base

glove

cleats

pitcher

Index